REINVENTING Your Work

8 Powerful Tips for a Joyful Career

CORINNE MILLER

Copyright © 2018 Corinne Miller

All rights reserved.

ISBN: 1986935701
ISBN-13: 978-1986935708

Illustrated by Betty Sitbon
bettysitbon@gmail.com

"Twenty years from now you will be more disappointed by the things that you didn't do than by the ones you did. So throw off the bowlines. Sail away from the safe harbor. Catch the trade winds in your sails. Explore. Dream. Discover."

H. Jackson Brown's mother from
P.S. I Love You: When Mom Wrote, She Always Saved the Best for Last

What's the Big Idea?

The more of your interests that you can integrate into your daily work, the more joy your work will bring you. This integration reinvents your work.

Reinventing your work is a simple but powerful concept. However, it's not always clear when, where, why, and how to do it. The journey twists and turns. Roadblocks will pop up. There will be pivotal decisions to be made.

This book presents eight tips to help you more easily reinvent your work, avoid issues, make better decisions, and enjoy your journey.

You'll need to recognize your interests to see where your opportunities lie. Create ways to integrate those interests into your daily work to feel fulfilled. Listen to the voice in your head for your compass and seek assistance from your support team. Find the courage to get past the fear and learning opportunities to inspire your creativity. Connect to your industry, field, and peers by giving back. And test the waters to reduce risk when you want to make a significant move.

A joyful worker is a higher performing worker. Everyone wins.

Reinventing8Tips.com

About This Book

Research tells us that we are joyful when we are creating in our areas of interest. When we do this, we are continuously growing, renewing, or as I like to call it, reinventing our work. I have done this for many years, and I can report that it has been indeed true for me whether I was reinventing within my current job or reinventing into a brand new career.

Frankly, I didn't really think much about this whole reinvention thing until people noticed my joy and kept asking me how I did it. So upon some deep reflection, I realized it's about focusing on the work, and eight powerful and practical tips clearly emerged.

This book is about my experiences that come from my corporate career and running my own small business. As such, while the eight tips can apply to anyone, they may especially resonate with those from similar professional environments. At any stage of your career, the eight tips apply.

Please note: The first page of each tip discussion is a general description; the second page includes examples from personal experience. I also included ideation questions for each tip to help you apply them. **Join the discussion and find more at: Reinventing8Tips.com.**

To the many who requested this book, thank you for the inspiration and with much gratitude to be able to pay the inspiration forward ... here we go.

Tip #1
Recognize Your Interests

The full range of our interests are not always evident to us. In fact, they can even change over time. We start our career in one area of interest but may not realize that we are multi-dimensional beings with many interests. It's important to know what these interests are and to integrate as many as possible into our daily work. This is where the joy lies.

You may be wondering why I am not mentioning passion. People cannot always make a living following their passion, so I have always encouraged focusing on one's areas of interest in the meantime until—or if—the passion route works out.

Our interests repeatedly express themselves in various forms throughout our lives, starting in childhood. Draw a roadmap of your professional and personal activities. Have fun with it. It doesn't need to be a work of art unless you want it to be. Look for interest patterns. Engage others who have known you for some time to help with drawing and analyzing the roadmap.

This is where you will find your OPPORTUNITY.

My personal roadmap showed that technology, art, travel, teaching, business, and innovation are interests that repeated throughout my life.

Despite how few or many years your roadmap covers, there are always interesting patterns to see.

Pull your roadmap out every six months and add to it. This will help you see your interests clearer and faster.

Career/Life Roadmap by Betty Sitbon

IDEATION QUESTIONS

1. Even with limited time, what activities do I make time for at work? To do? To discuss? To assist with?
2. What activities cause me to lose myself in thought?
3. What activities make me feel good?

Tip #2
Integrate Your Interests

Interests bring joy. With your list of interests from Tip #1 (Recognize Your Interests) in hand, check how many you are able to pursue or even touch upon in your current work. **The aim is to integrate as many interests as you can into your day-to-day work.**

Integration can be in small or large ways and doesn't have to be limited by the specifically assigned responsibilities of your current job. Integration serves both the worker and the employer well when done with an intent to improve or advance the current work or organization.

Sometimes, it just takes a little creative thought about how to do it. For example, if you have an interest in teaching and you're a financial analyst, perhaps you can be a mentor, help with onboarding, or train employees or customers.

If you find yourself gravitating more and more to one interest over the others, and it is not the focus of your day job, it might be time to reinvent to a new position.

This is where you will find your FULFILLMENT.

Technology has been a primary interest of mine for as long as I can remember. It's where I started my career. As such, I found ways to integrate technology into some of my "less technical" positions. For example, I create paintings containing a microchip that, when touched by a smartphone, displays a website explaining the painting.

An interest in business always led me to partner with finance and other business functions when I was in technology, quality, and training positions. I integrated business processes and metrics with the day-to-day work. Better business alignment and results were a win-win.

A lifelong interest in innovation, from childhood, was integrated into every bit of work I have ever done. Blending innovation principles into work processes, from human resources to manufacturing to product development work and more.

IDEATION QUESTIONS

1. How might I bring elements of [insert interests here] into my day job?
2. Who might be able to help me integrate my interests?
3. How might integrating my interests in [insert interests here] be of value to my organization?

Tip #3
Listen to the Voice in Your Head

There's a guiding voice in your head. Can you hear it? In today's busy world, it gets drowned out a lot. It will answer your questions about what to do, where and when to do it, with whom to do it, and how to do it.

In order to hear the voice, you need to make space for it in your head. Each person has a method that works for them, from a few minutes of daily meditation to thoughts that come during sleep.

Caution: Discouraging thoughts ahead. Sometimes, you will generate negative thoughts from fear and insecurity. Refocus on the guiding voice. That voice is always calm despite the message.

Messages may also appear fragmented. Write them down and organize them. This will especially help to weed out the unproductive ones.

Think back on when and where insightful thoughts have come to you. Make it a point to routinely allow these opportunities into your day to hear the all-important voice in your head.

This is where you will find your COMPASS.

The voice in my head can be heard when I lie in bed just after waking up in the morning, when I am writing in quiet, and as silly as it sounds, when I am engaged in mindless activities such as blow drying my hair. I hear the voice when I am alone as well as through conversations with other people. I had to learn to be very aware of the voice or I would miss it.

Others have told me that they hear the voice in the shower, on a train ride home from work, when in nature, walking, on bike rides—and even wandering up and down the aisles of their favorite store.

If the voice goes quiet, you need to go quiet. It will come back.

The voice isn't a voice different than your own. It's thoughts entering your mind that appear to be coming from outside of you. Sometimes, you wonder where they came from!

IDEATION QUESTIONS

1. When and where have great ideas popped into my head?
2. When and where did discouraging thoughts enter my mind?
3. What voice have I been ignoring?

Tip #4
Surround Yourself with Supportive People

Imagine a career surrounded by people who support you. Who is on your support team?

Garner support from people who can provide subject matter expertise, resources, inspiration, and prodding. What does this support look like? Those with expertise, who share their fully transparent opinion. Those who have the resources, including connections, to help you. Those who bring out the best in you. Those who can keep you moving forward.

The key is to mingle, network, connect and ask for assistance, and accept it with gratitude and without guilt.

Make a list of those who have provided support for you in the past, those who might be able to help now, anyone on your current support team who should be eliminated, and on who's support team you can contribute—expecting nothing in return.

This is where you will find your ASSISTANCE.

Some key lessons I learned about building and maintaining a support team over a career include:

- "Supportive" does not mean people who tell you what you want to hear to make you feel good.

- Not everyone's opinion counts. Unless the person has some expertise on the topic, I am not interested in their opinion. Expertise comes in many forms and I learned to recognize it, remove my biases, and relentlessly seek it out.

- I am always interested in every person's questions. I listen carefully to them and many times ask what is it they are really asking. These questions have provided great insight.

- It is natural that over time, we may accumulate some unsupportive people in our lives or outgrow relationships. Kindly move on from those who no longer fulfill a productive role.

IDEATION QUESTIONS

1. What type of support do I need?
2. Who might be willing to brainstorm with me?
3. To whom might I offer my support, expecting nothing in return?

Tip #5
Focus on Execution, Not Fear

Reinventing can be scary. Reinventing is about change, and change can incite fear as well as excitement. Some people find fear motivating, but many become procrastinators or even become immobilized.

Acknowledge your fear and move on with getting things done. Tell the fear that you have no space for it in your head. You need to fill that space with getting things done. With execution comes progress, feedback, engagement, learning, and inspiration to keep going. This is a great time to listen to the guiding voice in your head.

Identify ways to drive execution. For example, periodically review progress with a "prodder" from your support team; make scheduled commitments to specific individuals to show them each completed phase of your endeavor; and create a doable list of items that you can check off every week. Get so focused on execution that there is no room for fear.

This is where you will find your COURAGE.

To keep myself focused on execution, I acknowledge that I have fears. I don't beat myself up but rather tell myself that if others can do it, I can do it, too. Even if others have not done it, I can do it! Why not? What is the worst that can happen? And that's not so bad!

Not every step along the way will be fun and exciting. Procrastination will creep in when we are faced with a task we don't enjoy. Push through it as fast as possible while also doing some enjoyable things to fuel your motivation.

Take my first art show, for example. I had been painting for about a year and was doing well, but I certainly didn't have a great level of confidence. I decided to make a commitment to do a solo art show if an art gallery would have me. Talk about fear creeping in! So I showed the only two innovative paintings I had created with the microchip to a gallery who booked me for a show in one year. With this commitment, I spent the following year creating better and better paintings. I had no time for fear. I focused on execution, tapped into my support team, continued to learn, and the show was a success.

IDEATION QUESTIONS

1. If I had no constraints, what might I do?
2. What commitments might I make that are a stretch but won't break my spirit?
3. What actions should be on my list of things to do this week, next week, and next month?

Tip #6
Add to the Field

Maya Angelou said, "When you learn, teach. When you get, give." What can you teach or give back to your field or industry as a result of your experience, knowledge, and skills?

Sometimes, we think we don't have anything to offer. We might think we're not that brilliant or haven't achieved anything all that significant. Who would care what you have to say? I promise you that a lot of people do. You can help many and also grow yourself in doing so.

Everyone has something to offer. Give back. You know more than you think. Contributions can range from mentoring to authoring an article or book, contributing improved methods, training others, or speaking at a conference.

Start small with an area of your knowledge or skills that you feel you do well. Share or practice in a friendly environment first, (e.g., work colleagues, your support team). This will build your confidence to keep going.

This is where you will find your CONNECTION.

I started small with training others, especially since training is one of my interests. Then, I started writing articles and speaking about projects on which I was working. Later, I contributed chapters to published books and followed with my own book. I also teach as an adjunct faculty member at a graduate school.

People often tell me that they feel anxious about writing articles or speaking because of being potentially criticized or judged. While others could have had a different experience, who knows about your experience better than you? No one does. Share it with confidence and joy.

You never know who you will touch. Several years ago, I taught a class on telecommuting. Part of it was discussing ways to connect with others, to not feel so alone. It was a good class, but I didn't think anything of it until I ran into a participant a few years later. They told me that the tips helped them deal with the loneliness that was causing suicidal thoughts. I felt so humbled and blessed. What you might see as inconsequential could help others in small and large ways.

IDEATION QUESTIONS

1. Who could benefit from my knowledge, skills, or experience?
2. What unique experiences have I had that give me insight I can share?
3. In what mediums might I share my knowledge?

Tip #7
Always Seek New Experiences, Knowledge & Skills

New understandings spur reinvention. We cannot continually reinvent our work unless we are always seeking new experiences, knowledge, and skills. This is how our interests, creativity, and inspiration grow.

In a busy world, it often seems overwhelming to take the time to learn new things. **Size learning opportunities to fit into your life, but stretch and force yourself through times when you're less motivated.**

There's a famous saying to question everything. Don't. There isn't enough time. Your assumptions are your biggest blind spot and what should be constantly questioned. Force yourself to identify and question your assumptions. This will lead to pivotal learning.

Learning opportunities can range from a lunch-time webinar to a new job, attending or presenting at a meeting, collaborations, researching an area of interest, practicing a new skill, earning an educational certificate or degree, or transitioning to a new career.

This is where you will find your CREATIVITY.

I have found three types of people: those who are avid learners, those who learn only when they have to, and those who are comfortable where they are and have no interest in going beyond it. Which one are you?

I'm an avid learner. I find ways to learn new things despite how busy I am. The techniques I use are spending an hour at lunch or a break; meeting with smart people for lunch and coffee; taking a class (online and in-person); immersing myself by very quickly reading a bunch of books on a topic; and seriously considering the feedback of skilled people. I am an incessant Googler every time something pops into my head that I want to know more about.

I have had a few disruptive learning experiences, meaning they led to a pivotal reinvention in my work. These include earning a Master of Science in Communication degree late in my career; temporarily leaving the technology field to run a bowling ball company; and hiring a master artist for three 14-hour days of one-on-one immersion training.

IDEATION QUESTIONS

1. What am I interested in learning more about?
2. What do I know for sure, and how might I question this certainty?
3. How might I integrate my insights into my work?

> **Tip #8**
Transition with One Foot in Each Pond

A new adventure awaits. **Test the waters first to scale your risk.** For significant job changes, this will reduce stress. A calmer mind can more clearly receive a guiding voice and make good decisions.

While it is not always possible, the best way to explore whether a significant job change is best at this time is to rely on your experience from Tip #2 (Integrate Your Interests). When you can actually perform some of the work of a future job in your current work, it's a great way to decide whether it is right for you. If it's not possible, seek out an opportunity from a professional or volunteer organization.

Engage your support team and others working in your area of interest to offer suggestions on organizations, with whom you might network, and how you might prepare yourself. Keep Tip #5 (Focus on Execution, Not Fear) in mind to get past the fear of never feeling completely ready.

This is where you will find your ADVENTURE.

I've made some interesting job transitions. From small to large companies, from high-tech to low-tech, from engineering to the sports industry to human resources to trainer to artist.

Every time I made a significant change, I performed a sample of the work from the next job in the current job. For example, before moving from engineering to a learning and development (L&D) function, I partnered with the L&D team on projects for my organization. I got to know the work and the people. I left engineering a year later to join the L&D team.

Another thing that has served me well is that I deeply immerse myself in the new work to learn it fast. Before and after I moved to L&D, I read every piece of material recommended to me by experts, enlisted a few informal coaches highly skilled and connected in L&D, and took some online classes. This—in addition to the experience of trying out the work before the move—gave me the jumpstart I needed to be a contributing and respected member of the new team.

IDEATION QUESTIONS

1. Who might help me check my thinking about this move?
2. Who might help me make a move?
3. How might I be as fully prepared as is reasonable?

REINVENTING Your Work

EIGHT TIPS QUICK SUMMARY

	Tip	Key Thought	Gift
1	RECOGNIZE YOUR INTERESTS	Interests repeatedly express themselves in various forms throughout our lives, starting in childhood.	OPPORTUNITY
2	INTEGRATE YOUR INTERESTS	Integrate as many interests as you can into your daily work.	FULFILLMENT
3	LISTEN TO THE VOICE IN YOUR HEAD	Make space for the voice in your head.	COMPASS
4	SURROUND YOURSELF WITH SUPPORTIVE PEOPLE	Garner support that provides expertise, inspiration, resources, and prodding.	ASSISTANCE
5	FOCUS ON EXECUTION, NOT FEAR	Acknowledge your fear and move on with getting things done.	COURAGE
6	ADD TO THE FIELD	Everyone has something to offer. Give back.	CONNECTION
7	ALWAYS SEEK NEW EXPERIENCES, KNOWLEDGE & SKILLS	Size learning to fit your life, but stretch and force yourself when less motivated.	CREATIVITY
8	TRANSITION WITH ONE FOOT IN EACH POND	Test the waters to reduce risk.	ADVENTURE

Reinventing8Tips.com

Be the Person to Go for It!

As Dr. Seuss said in, "Oh the Places You Will Go" …
"You will come to a place where the streets are not marked.
Some windows are lighted. But mostly they're darked.
A place you could sprain both your elbow and your chin!
Do you dare to stay out? Do you dare to go in?
How much can you lose? How much can you win?"

Thank You

To those who have provided expertise,
inspiration, resources,
and even some prodding.

(In chronological order)

Carmen & Ginny Salvino

George Miller

Vern Hamlin

Barbara Hirsh

John Cipolla

Kathleen Galvin

Fred Harburg

Dirk Tussing

Kathy Leck

Carrie Buchwald

Betty Sitbon

About the Author

At three years old during a dance class, Corinne Miller insisted that the teacher play faster music for her to dance to. She then proceeded to dance across the floor, alone, in her own way. Nothing has changed.

InnovatingResults.com
InnovatingArtwork.com
LinkedIn.com/in/CorinneMiller

● ● ●

Reinventing8Tips.com

www.ingramcontent.com/pod-product-compliance
Lightning Source LLC
Chambersburg PA
CBHW051836210526
45473CB00005B/1904